Rhode Island

BY ANN HEINRICHS

Content Adviser: Elizabeth Fitzgerald, Providence Public Library, Providence, Rhode Island

Reading Adviser: Dr. Linda D. Labbo, Department of Reading Education, College of Education, The University of Georgia

COMPASS POINT BOOKS MINNEAPOLIS, MINNESOTA

Compass Point Books
3109 West 50th Street, #115
Minneapolis, MN 55410

Visit Compass Point Books on the Internet at *www.compasspointbooks.com*
or e-mail your request to *custserv@compasspointbooks.com*

On the cover: Sakonnet Lighthouse

Photographs ©: Corbis/Onne van der Wal, cover, 1, 29; Unicorn Stock Photos/Patti McConville, 3, 8;
Unicorn Stock Photos/Thomas H. Mitchell, 5, 38, 40, 48 (top); Photo Network/Jeff Greenberg, 6; North
Wind Picture Archives, 9, 14, 15, 16, 17, 18; James P. Rowan, 10, 37, 41, 43 (top); Robert McCaw, 11,
42, 44 (top, middle); Corbis/Kevin Fleming, 12; Hulton/Archive by Getty Images, 13, 30 (bottom), 31
(top), 46; Hulton-Deutsch Collection/Corbis, 19; Unicorn Stock Photos/Andre Jenny, 20, 24, 31 (bottom),
45, 47; Photo Network/D & I Mac Donald, 21; Photo Network/Jim Schwabel, 23, 35; Corbis/David H.
Wells, 25; Corbis/Robert Dowling, 26; Index Stock Imagery/Kindra Clineff, 27; Photo Network/Patti
McConville, 28, 36; Corbis/Reuters NewMedia Inc., 30 (top); Corbis/Lee Snider; Lee Snider, 32;
Corbis/David Muench, 34; Courtesy of Rhode Island Tourism Division, 39; Robesus, Inc., 43 (state flag);
One Mile Up, Inc., 43 (state seal); Comstock, 44 (bottom).

Editors: E. Russell Primm, Emily J. Dolbear, and Patricia Stockland
Photo Researcher: Marcie C. Spence
Photo Selector: Linda S. Koutris
Designer: The Design Lab
Cartographer: XNR Productions, Inc.

Library of Congress Cataloging-in-Publication Data
Heinrichs, Ann.
  Rhode Island / by Ann Heinrichs.
      p. cm. — (This land is your land)
 Summary: Introduces the geography, history, government, people, culture, and attractions of Rhode
Island. Includes bibliographical references (p.) and index.
  ISBN 0-7565-0358-2 (alk. paper)
  1. Rhode Island—Juvenile literature. [1. Rhode Island.] I. Title. II. Series.
  F79.3.H456 2004
  974.5—dc21   2003005412

Table of Contents

NOTE: In this book, words that are defined in the glossary are in **bold** *the first time they appear in the text.*

Roger Williams had "dangerous opinions." That's what the Massachusetts Bay **Colony** decided in 1635. The colony forced him to leave. Williams left and founded Providence. This **settlement** was the beginning of the Rhode Island Colony.

Williams's most "dangerous opinion" was religious freedom. He believed that "forced worship stinks in God's nostrils." In Rhode Island, people of all faiths were welcome. The **colonists** made their own laws and governed themselves. Later, Rhode Island was the first colony to declare independence from Great Britain.

Tiny Rhode Island is the smallest state. However, its ideals became basic principles of the United States. Rhode Island is also the birthplace of our nation's factory system. Its water-powered mills were America's first factories.

Rhode Island's nickname is the Ocean State. Hundreds of miles of coastline face the Atlantic Ocean and Narragansett Bay. Millionaires have built huge mansions overlooking the sea. Today, visitors enjoy fishing, boating, and swimming along the sandy beaches. Now let's explore Rhode Island—a small state with a big impact on us all!

▲ A Portsmouth lighthouse along Narragansett Bay

Water, Water, Everywhere

Look at a map of the United States. Can you pick out Rhode Island? On many maps, you can hardly see it! Rhode Island is the smallest of the fifty states. It could fit inside Alaska, the largest state, 424 times! Because it's so small, Rhode Island is sometimes called Little Rhody.

▲ **Providence is Rhode Island's largest city.**

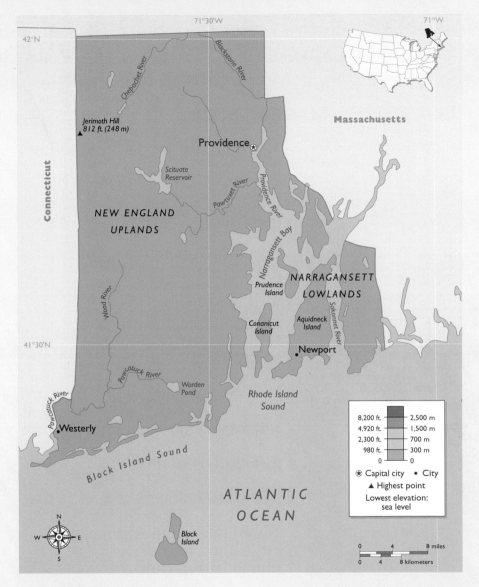

71°30'W   71°W

42°N

Massachusetts

Jerimoth Hill
▲ 812 ft. (248 m)

Providence ✪

Scituate
Reservoir

NEW ENGLAND
UPLANDS

Chepachet River

Blackstone River

Pawtuxet River

Providence River

Narragansett Bay

NARRAGANSETT
LOWLANDS

Prudence
Island

Wood River

Conanicut
Island

Aquidneck
Island

Sakonnet River

41°30'N

Pawcatuck River

Worden
Pond

Newport

Pawcatuck River

• Westerly

Rhode Island
Sound

8,200 ft.	2,500 m
4,920 ft.	1,500 m
2,300 ft.	700 m
980 ft.	300 m
0	0

✪ Capital city   • City
▲ Highest point
Lowest elevation:
sea level

Block Island Sound

ATLANTIC
OCEAN

Block
Island

| 0 | 4 | 8 miles |
| 0 | 4 | 8 kilometers |

N
W   E
S

▲ **A topographic map of Rhode Island**

Rhode Island is one of the New England states. It's
located in the northeast section of the United States.
Massachusetts borders Rhode Island to the north and east.

▲ Bowen's Wharf is located in
Newport, one of Rhode Island's
major cities.

Connecticut lies to the west. Southern Rhode Island faces the Atlantic Ocean.

Narragansett Bay cuts deeply into Rhode Island. It almost divides the state in two. This waterway is an arm of the Atlantic Ocean. At the head of the bay is Providence, the capital and largest city.

Many islands lie in Narragansett Bay. Some of these islands are just clusters of rocks. The largest island is Aquidneck Island. In the 1600s, this island was named Rhode Island. Now the whole state is called by that name. Newport and Portsmouth are major cities on Aquidneck Island. Block Island lies a few miles south of the mainland.

The Blackstone River flows through northeastern Rhode Island. Many mills, or water-powered factories, sprang up along the Blackstone. Pawtucket is the major city on this river. The Blackstone's waters eventually flow into Narragansett Bay.

▲ **Textile mills along the Blackstone River in Pawtucket**

▲ Rocky cliffs on a beach in Newport

Eastern Rhode Island lies in the Narragansett Lowlands, or Coastal Lowlands. It includes land east and west of the bay and its islands. Sandy beaches and rocky cliffs line the shores. The mainland's southern coast has many ponds and wetlands.

Western Rhode Island lies within the New England Upland. Here the land rises higher, forming rocky, forested hills. Several lakes and ponds are nestled among the hills.

Forests cover more than half of the state. Rabbits, wood-chucks, raccoons, and beavers make their homes there. Many water birds live along the shores. They include gulls, ospreys, and ducks. The wetlands are home to long-legged herons, too.

Lobsters, clams, mussels, and oysters live in the coastal waters. The shell of the quahog, a type of clam, is the state shell. Both saltwater and freshwater fish are found in Narragansett Bay. The bay receives saltwater from the ocean and freshwater from rivers.

Rhode Island gets all kinds of weather. Hurricanes with their fierce winds may strike in the summer and fall. Winter can bring ice storms and heavy snows. Near the coasts, however,

▲ Ospreys live along Rhode Island's shoreline.

▲ **A snowy winter day in Wickford**

summers are cooler and winters are warmer than they are
inland. The waters of the ocean and the bay are like a cush-
ion. They shield the coastal areas from extreme temperatures.

Rhode Island was once home to many Native Americans. The largest group was the Narragansett. Villages of related families lived in bark huts. Village leaders were called **sachems.** The men caught fish and shellfish in the rivers and coastal waters. They hunted in the forests. Women planted and harvested corn, beans, and squash. Other groups in the region included the Wampanoag, Nipmuc, and Niantic.

Giovanni da Verrazano was the first European to reach Rhode Island. He was an Italian sailor working for France. Verrazano explored Narragansett Bay

▲ **A Narragansett chief**

in 1524. In 1614, the Dutchman Adriaen Block landed on present-day Block Island. Verrazano had originally named the island Claudia.

Roger Williams established Providence in 1636. It was Rhode Island's first permanent settlement. Williams was a minister in the Puritan faith. However, he strongly believed in religious freedom. He also believed in treating the Native Americans fairly.

Other settlements soon sprang up nearby. They were united as one colony in 1663. Unfortunately, settlers often clashed with their Native American neighbors. In 1676, settlers defeated the Native Americans in King Philip's War.

Most Rhode Islanders were farmers. They raised

▲ Giovanni da Verrazano was the first European to explore Rhode Island.

▲ European settlers fought with Native Americans during King Philip's War.

crops, cattle, and horses. African slaves worked on many of the larger farms. In 1784, a law passed that freed the children of female slaves. However, the slave trade remained a major part of Rhode Island's economy for many years.

Rhode Island was one of thirteen colonies ruled by Great Britain. Like other colonists, Rhode Islanders wanted to be

▲ Colonists burning a British ship in Providence Harbor shortly before the Revolutionary War

free. They declared their independence on May 4, 1776. The other colonies soon followed. The colonies signed the Declaration of Independence on July 4. The colonists finally won their freedom in the Revolutionary War (1775–1783).

The United States drew up a Constitution, or basic set of laws. One by one, the former colonies ratified, or approved, the Constitution. Each one became a U.S. state when it voted yes. However, Rhode Islanders insisted that the Constitution include additional rights that would limit the government's power and protect individuals. The Bill of Rights was added, and Rhode Island was satisfied. It became the thirteenth U.S. state in 1790.

Manufacturing quickly became Rhode Island's major **industry.** In 1790, Samuel Slater built a water-powered cloth mill in Pawtucket. As its giant wheel turned, the parts in the factory's machines moved. Soon, many **textile** mills opened alongside the rivers. Rhode Islanders made fine jewelry and silver items, too. Some people worked in the whaling industry. Oil and fat from the whales were made into candles.

By the early 1800s, thousands of mill workers

▲ Men at work on a whaling boat during the 1800s

lived in the cities. However, landowners outside the cities had more voice in their government than these citizens. Thomas Dorr and his followers staged the Dorr Rebellion in 1842. After that, all citizens were given fairer voting rights.

Rhode Island's textile industry slowed down in the early 1900s. Many mills moved to southern states, where labor was cheaper. New factories began making machines, tools, and other metal products. These goods were useful in World War II (1939–1945). The Quonset Point Navy base made another contribution to the war—quonset huts. These long sheet-metal buildings stored military supplies.

After the war, business declined again. By 1949, at least one out of six workers was unemployed. Again, new industries sprang up. Rhode

▲ **Thomas Dorr staged a rebellion in 1842 to give Rhode Islanders fairer voting rights.**

Island branched out into electronics, chemicals, and plastics. Tourism was a growing industry in the 1960s and 1970s. Visitors could travel over the Newport Bridge and Interstate Highway 95.

▲ Sailors who served in World War II sometimes trained at the U.S. Naval Training Station in Newport. This photograph, taken in 1940, shows recruits studying a scale model of a ship they will be stationed aboard.

Today, Rhode Island is one of the nation's most industrial states. It's also an important center for ocean research. "Little Rhody" has big hopes for the future.

▲ **Newport Bridge in Narragansett Bay**

Rhode Island, the smallest state, has the longest official name. It's the State of Rhode Island and Providence Plantations. The name comes from colonial times. Only Aquidneck Island, including the towns of Newport, Portsmouth, and Middletown, was originally called Rhode Island. Providence Plantations included the town of Providence and the rest of the state. When all of these towns united, they ended up with quite a long name!

Freedom has always been important to Rhode Islanders. The colonists enjoyed self-rule and religious freedom. They were the first to declare independence in 1776. Today the state capitol in Providence displays a symbol of these ideals. On top of this government building is a statue called the Independent Man.

▲ The state capitol in Providence

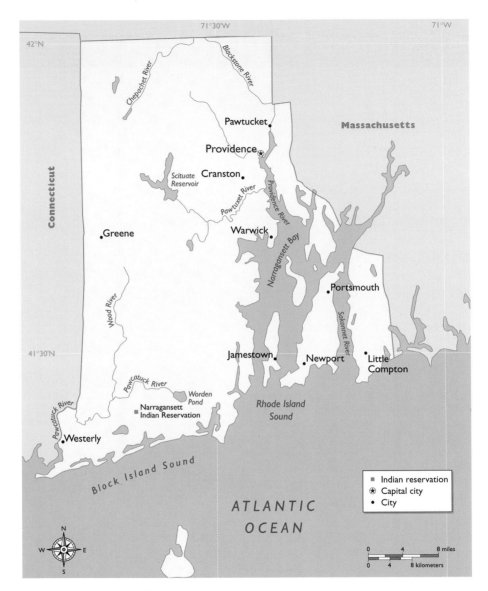

71°30'W   71°W

42°N

Chepachet River

Blackstone River

Connecticut

Pawtucket

Providence

Scituate Reservoir

Cranston

Pawtuxet River

Greene

Providence River

Warwick

Narragansett Bay

Massachusetts

Wood River

Portsmouth

Sakonnet River

41°30'N

Pawcatuck River

Jamestown

Newport

Little Compton

Worden Pond

Rhode Island Sound

Narragansett Indian Reservation

Pawcatuck River

Westerly

Block Island Sound

ATLANTIC OCEAN

■ Indian reservation
✹ Capital city
• City

N W E S

0   4   8 miles
0   4   8 kilometers

▲ **A geopolitical map of Rhode Island**

Rhode Island has three branches of state government—legislative, executive, and judicial. This is a good way to preserve the citizens' freedom. Each branch makes sure the others do not become too powerful.

The legislative branch makes the state laws. Voters elect their lawmakers to serve in the General Assembly. It has two houses, or parts—a 50-member senate and a 100-member house of representatives.

The executive branch carries out the state's laws. Rhode Island's governor heads the executive branch.

▲ State senators meet in this chamber in the capitol.

Voters choose a governor every four years. The governor may serve only two terms in a row. Voters also elect four other executive officers.

The judicial branch decides whether someone has broken a law. Rhode Island's highest court is the state supreme court. It has five justices, or judges.

▲ Judges decide cases in this Providence courthouse.

Rhode Island is divided into five counties. Each county has a sheriff and courts, but counties do not have any other responsibilities. Cities and towns take care of local government. Rhode Island has eight cities and thirty-one towns. Most cities elect a mayor and a city council. In most towns, people hold a town meeting once a year. They elect officials, vote on laws, and take care of other town business. As always, the people insist on their independence!

Rhode Island is called the birthplace of the American factory system. Its textile mills were the nation's first modern factories. Many Rhode Island industries that exist today had their beginnings in the 1700s. Jewelry, silver, textile, and metalworking are some of these industries.

Rhode Island is known for its beautiful jewelry and silverware. Other factory goods from Rhode Island include computer parts, electrical equipment, metal goods, machines, and scientific instruments. Textiles are still made, too.

▲ **Thread spindles on a loom at a textile mill in Pawtucket**

Rhode Islanders make fine lace, as well as yarn, wool, and knitted clothes.

Rhode Island does not have much farmland. Its top farm goods are greenhouse and nursery products. These include decorative flowers, shrubs, and trees. Milk is also a valuable farm product. Some farmers raise potatoes, hay, and corn. Apples are the state's leading fruit.

The Rhode Island Red is the state bird. It's a type of chicken raised in Little Compton. Rhode Island Reds are called dual-purpose chickens. They're tasty to eat and good egg-layers, too. One chicken lays between two hundred and three hundred eggs a year.

Rhode Island is a great fishing state. Lobsters are the most

▲ The state bird is the Rhode Island Red.

valuable catch. Have you ever eaten squid? It's another important catch. Try it—it's delicious and crunchy when deep-fried!
Fishers also haul in quahogs, cod, flounder, mackerel, and
other fish.

Service industries are important to the state's economy.
Service workers are paid for their services instead of their
products. Some work in banks, schools, hospitals, or stores.
Others may program computers or repair things. Most service
jobs are in Providence and other big cities.

▲ **Fishing boats docked at Point Judith off of Block Island**

▲ **A Narragansett Indian monument**

Rhode Islanders are tightly packed into their little state. Only New Jersey has more people per square mile. About six out of seven Rhode Islanders live in city areas. Providence is the largest city. Next in size are Warwick, Cranston, and Pawtucket.

In 2000, there were 1,048,319 people in Rhode Island. That made it forty-third in population among all the states. Nine American cities have a larger population than all of Rhode Island!

Most Rhode Islanders are descendants of Europeans. About one out of twenty residents is African-American. Asians, **Hispanics**, and Native Americans live in Rhode Island, too. In 1975, Narragansett Indians sued the state for the return of their lands. They received about 1,800 acres (728 hectares) around Charlestown. Today the Narragansett **reservation** is located there.

Rhode Island's biggest events are boat races and fishing contests. The Newport-Bermuda **Yacht** Race is in June. July brings the Block Island Sound Race. The America's Cup yacht race takes off from Newport, too. Fishing contests include the Atlantic Tuna Tournament and the Rhode Island Open Salt-Water Fishing Derby.

The Newport Winter Festival usually lasts for ten days in February. People come to enjoy ice-skating, food, and music.

▲ **Sailboats compete in the Block Island Sound Race.**

▲ Singer Bob Dylan performing at the Apple and Eve Newport Folk Music Festival

▲ Gilbert Stuart painting his famous portrait of George Washington

Newport is also a great spot for music events. The Newport Music Festival features classical musicians performing in beautiful Newport mansions. Newport holds jazz and folk festivals, too.

You may not know it, but you're familiar with a Rhode Island artist. You probably see his work every day. He's Gilbert Stuart. He painted the most famous portrait of George Washington. The face from that picture is on the United States' one-dollar bills!

Many other Rhode Islanders became famous, as well. They are actor Harry Anderson and news show host David Hartman. George M. Cohan wrote tunes such as "Yankee Doodle Dandy" and "Give My Regards to Broadway." H. P. Lovecraft was known for writing mystery stories.

The Rhode Island School of Design is located in Providence. It's one of the best art and design schools in the country. Rhode Island College was founded in Providence in 1764. It grew into today's Brown University. Newport is the home of the Naval War College. U.S. Navy officers get advanced training there.

▲ Rhode Islander George M. Cohan was a famous songwriter.

▲ Carrie Tower is located on the campus of Brown University.

First Baptist Church in Providence

Rhode Island is a great place to explore history and enjoy nature. In Providence, the white-marble statehouse overlooks the city. Inside, you'll see the original charter that made Rhode Island a colony. You'll also see Gilbert Stuart's famous painting of George Washington.

Providence's First Baptist Church was built in 1775. It's America's oldest Baptist church. Baptists trace their history back to Roger Williams. He founded the first Baptist group in 1638. Providence's Benefit Street is often

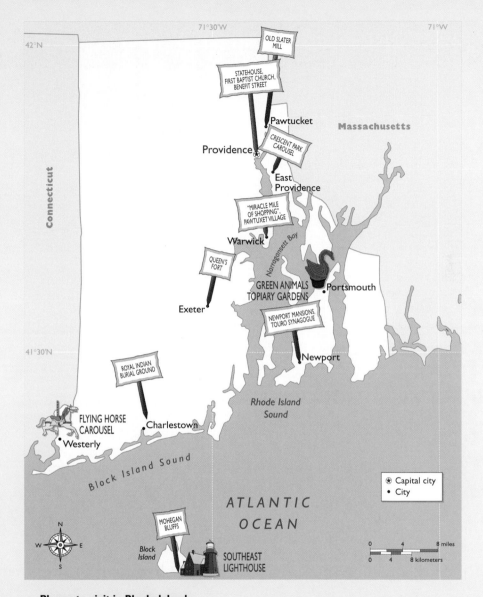

71°30'W   71°W

42°N

OLD SLATER MILL

STATEHOUSE, FIRST BAPTIST CHURCH, BENEFIT STREET

Pawtucket

Massachusetts

Connecticut

CRESCENT PARK CAROUSEL

Providence

East Providence

"MIRACLE MILE OF SHOPPING", PAWTUXET VILLAGE

Warwick

Narragansett Bay

QUEEN'S FORT

GREEN ANIMALS TOPIARY GARDENS

Portsmouth

Exeter

NEWPORT MANSIONS, TOURO SYNAGOGUE

41°30'N

Newport

ROYAL INDIAN BURIAL GROUND

Rhode Island Sound

FLYING HORSE CAROUSEL

Charlestown

Westerly

Block Island Sound

⊛ Capital city
• City

ATLANTIC OCEAN

N
W   E
S

MOHEGAN BLUFFS

Block Island

SOUTHEAST LIGHTHOUSE

0   4   8 miles
0   4   8 kilometers

▲ **Places to visit in Rhode Island**

called the Mile of History. Several old colonial buildings stand

along the street. These include the Providence Athenaeum

and the John Brown House.

▲ **A beach along Narragansett Bay**

You'll find a different kind of "mile" in Warwick. It's the "Miracle Mile of Shopping." Warwick is famous for its many shops and discount stores. The city's Pawtuxet Village preserves a famous colonial site. Colonists burned the British ship *Gaspée* offshore in 1772.

Many kinds of wildlife live around Narragansett Bay. Oysters, clams, lobsters, and sea stars are found along the shore. Ducks paddle by, and gulls soar overhead. In the winter, seals lounge on the rocks offshore. People take special nature tours just to see them.

Would you like to see a shrub shaped like a teddy bear, elephant, or giraffe? Just visit Green Animals Topiary Gardens in Portsmouth. Topiary is the art of forming trees and shrubs into interesting shapes. This garden has eighty pieces of shrub art, including twenty-one animals.

What do you imagine when you hear "summer cottages"? Whatever you picture, it's probably nothing like the Newport mansions. Wealthy people built these summer homes in the late 1800s. You can

▲ Shrub sculptures at the Green Animals Topiary Gardens in Portsmouth

▲ **The Breakers in Newport was designed to resemble an Italian palace.**

visit many of them today. They are more like palaces than cottages! One is the seventy-room Breakers. It was built to look like an Italian palace. The Astors' Beechwood offers living-history tours. Its costumed actors re-create the lifestyle of the original residents.

Newport's Touro Synagogue is the oldest Jewish synagogue in North America. It was built in 1763. Jewish people were welcomed in Rhode Island. The colony granted religious freedom to all.

You can ride a ferry to Block Island. Once you're there, you can explore the island's several nature trails. For a great sea view, walk along Mohegan Bluffs. These cliffs loom high above the southern shore. At one point, you'll come

▲ **Touro Synagogue in Newport**

▲ Southeast Lighthouse is located on Block Island.

to Southeast Lighthouse. It has one of the brightest light beams on the East Coast.

The Narragansett Indian Reservation surrounds Charlestown. Within the reservation is the Royal Indian Burial Ground. There you can visit the graves of many Narragansett chiefs and their families. The Narragansett longhouse was once the meeting place for tribal members.

Queen's Fort in Exeter is an old Narragansett fort. It's named for a female sachem. Native Americans took refuge here after the Great Swamp Fight of 1675. That battle occurred during King Philip's War.

Do you like riding merry-go-rounds? They're also called carousels. Rhode Island has many famous old carousels. One is the Flying Horse Carousel in Westerly. It was built in 1867 and may be America's oldest carousel. The horses hang from above and "fly out" as it turns. Also try the Crescent Park Carousel in East Providence. The horses were handmade by Charles Looff, a great carousel artist.

How did textile mills turn cotton into cloth? You

▲ A horse on the Crescent Park Carousel (Looff Carousel) located in East Providence

▲ **Old Slater Mill in Pawtucket**

can watch the whole process at Old Slater Mill in Pawtucket. Samuel Slater built this mill in 1793. First you'll see its huge waterwheel. Inside, you'll watch the machinery spin thread and weave cloth. Then count your blessings because children as young as six years old used to work here!

Rhode Island may be the smallest state, but it is filled with many amazing historic sites and natural attractions. Once you visit the Ocean State, you'll want to come back again and again.

Important Dates

1524   The Italian navigator Giovanni da Verrazano sails into Narragansett Bay.

1614   The Dutch navigator Adriaen Block lands on what is now Block Island.

1636   Puritan leader Roger Williams establishes Providence, Rhode Island's first settlement.

1638   William Coddington and others establish Portsmouth on Aquidneck Island.

1647   Providence, Portsmouth, Newport, and Warwick are united as the Rhode Island Colony.

1676   Settlers defeat the Native Americans in King Philip's War.

1764   Rhode Island College is founded and will eventually become Brown University.

1784   Rhode Island passes a law freeing the children of female slaves. It did not free all slaves, however.

1790   Rhode Island becomes the thirteenth U.S. state on May 29; Samuel Slater builds America's first water-powered textile mill in Pawtucket.

1842   Thomas Dorr leads the Dorr Rebellion; it leads to reforms in state government.

1900   Providence officially becomes the state capital.

1938   A hurricane causes terrible damage along Rhode Island's coastal areas.

1969   Newport Bridge is completed over Narragansett Bay; it connects Newport and Jamestown.

1990   Rhode Islanders celebrate their 200th anniversary as a state.

1991   Hurricane Bob causes millions of dollars' worth of damage.

2001   A partnership between industries and the government is launched to restore Rhode Island's wetlands.

Glossary

colonists—people who settle a new land for their home country

colony—a territory that belongs to the country that settles it

Hispanics—people of Mexican, South American, and other Spanish-speaking cultures

industry—a business or trade

reservation—a large area of land set aside for Native Americans

sachems—Native American village chiefs and religious leaders

settlement—a new town or village

textile—cloth

yacht—a very large recreational boat

Did You Know?

★ There are two stories about the origin of Rhode Island's name. One is that Giovanni da Verrazano saw Block Island and said it looked like the Greek island of Rhodes. The other story is that Dutch explorer Adriaen Block saw the red clay shores of Aquidneck Island. He named it *Roodt Eylandt,* which is Dutch for "red island."

★ The toy Mr. Potato Head was invented in Pawtucket.

★ Rhode Island was the first original colony to declare independence and the last to become a state.

★ New England consists of six states— Rhode Island, Massachusetts, New Hampshire, Vermont, Connecticut, and Maine

At a Glance

Official name: State of Rhode Island and Providence Plantations

State capital: Providence

State motto: Hope

State nickname: Ocean State

Statehood: May 29, 1790; thirteenth state

Land area: 1,045 square miles (2,707 square kilometers); **rank:** fiftieth

Highest point: Jerimoth Hill, 812 feet (248 meters) above sea level

Lowest point: Sea level along the Atlantic coast

Highest recorded temperature: 104°F (40°C) at Providence on August 2, 1975

Lowest recorded temperature: −25°F (−32°C) at Greene on February 5, 1996

Average January temperature: 29°F (−2°C)

Average July temperature: 71°F (22°C)

Population in 2000: 1,048,319; **rank:** forty-third

Largest cities in 2000: Providence (173,618), Warwick (85,808), Cranston (79,269), Pawtucket (72,958)

Factory products: Jewelry, silverware, metal products, electrical and electronics equipment

Farm products: Greenhouse and nursery products, milk, potatoes

Mining products: Granite, sand, gravel

Fishery products: Lobsters, clams, squid

State flag: Rhode Island's state flag shows a gold anchor on a white background. The anchor is a symbol of hope. The white background stands for Rhode Island soldiers who fought and died in the Revolutionary War. Thirteen gold stars are arranged in a circle around the anchor. They stand for the thirteen original colonies. Beneath the anchor is a blue banner with the state motto, Hope.

State seal: The state seal includes the flag's anchor symbol and motto banner. At the bottom is the date 1636. That was the year Roger Williams founded the settlement of Providence.

State abbreviations: R.I. (traditional); RI (postal)

State Symbols

State bird: Rhode Island Red chicken

State flower: Violet

State tree: Red maple

State fish: Striped bass

State fruit: Rhode Island Greening apple

State mineral: Bowenite

State rock: Cumberlandite

State shell: Quahog

State drink: Coffee milk

State flagship: *Providence*

State yacht: *Courageous*

Making Johnnycakes

These cornmeal pancakes, sometimes called johnnycakes, are a traditional Rhode Island food.

Makes about ten johnnycakes.

INGREDIENTS:

2 cups cornmeal

1 tablespoon sugar

1 teaspoon salt

1/4 cup boiling water

1 cup milk

Vegetable oil

Butter or margarine

Syrup

DIRECTIONS:

Make sure an adult helps you with the hot stove and boiling water. Mix cornmeal, sugar, and salt in a large mixing bowl. Add boiling water and stir. Then stir in the milk right away. Mixture should be thick but still a little runny. If it's too thick, just add a little more milk. Put a very thin layer of vegetable oil in a skillet or griddle and heat it. For each pancake, drop large spoonfuls of batter onto the hot pan. Cook until the bottom is lightly browned (about 3-4 minutes). Turn and brown the other side. Serve with butter or margarine and syrup.

"Rhode Island's It for Me"

Words by Charlie Hall, music by Maria Day

I've been to every state we have,
and I think that I'm inclined to say
that Rhody stole my heart:
You can keep the forty-nine.

Herring gulls that dot the sky,
blue waves that paint the rocks,
waters rich with Neptune's life,
the boats that line the docks.
I see the lighthouse flickering
to help the sailors see.
There's a place for everyone:
Rhode Island's it for me.

Chorus:
Rhode Island, oh, Rhode Island
surrounded by the sea.
Some people roam the earth for home;
Rhode Island's it for me.

I love the fresh October days,
the buzz of College Hill,
art that moves an eye to tear,
a jeweler's special skill.
Icicles refract the sun,
snow falling gracefully.
Some search for a place that's warm:
Rhode Island's it for me.

The skyline piercing Providence,
the State House dome so rare,
residents who speak their minds;
no longer unaware!
Roger Williams would be proud
to see his colony,
so don't sell short this precious port:
Rhode Island's it for me.

Harry Anderson (1951–) is an actor and magician. He appeared on the television comedy *Night Court.* Anderson was born in Newport.

George M. Cohan (1878–1942) was an actor and composer. He was famous for musical comedies. Cohan (pictured above left) wrote "Yankee Doodle Dandy" and "Give My Regards to Broadway." He was born in Providence.

Nelson Eddy (1901–1967) was a popular singer in the 1930s and 1940s. He often appeared in movies with singer Jeanette MacDonald. Eddy was born in Johnston.

Robert Gray (1755–1806) was a sea captain and explorer. He was the first American to sail around the world. Gray was born in Newport.

Spalding Gray (1941–) is an actor and writer. He is best known for appearing in *Swimming to Cambodia* (1987). Gray was born in Barrington.

David Hartman (1935–) is a television news reporter and host. He appeared for several years on *Good Morning America.* Hartman was born in Pawtucket.

Julia Ward Howe (1819–1910) was a social reformer and poet. She wrote the words to "The Battle Hymn of the Republic." She was born in New York and later lived in Rhode Island.

Van Johnson (1916–) is an actor. His movies include *Brigadoon* (1954) and *The Caine Mutiny* (1954). Johnson was born in Newport.

H. P. Lovecraft (1890–1937) was a writer of weird mystery and science-fiction stories. H. P. stands for Howard Phillips. He was born in Providence.

Matthew Perry (1794–1858) was a U.S. Navy officer. He led a mission in 1853 to open up U.S. relations with Japan. He was the brother of Oliver Perry (below). Perry was born in South Kingston.

Oliver Hazard Perry (1785–1819) was a U.S. Navy officer. He won the Battle of Lake Erie in the War of 1812 (1812–1814). Perry was born in South Kingston.

Samuel Slater (1768–1835) is called the Father of American Industry. He built Rhode Island's first water-powered textile mill in Pawtucket. Slater was born in England.

Gilbert Stuart (1755–1828) was an artist. He painted the famous portrait of George Washington that now appears on the United States' one-dollar bill. Stuart was born in Saunderstown.

Roger Williams (1603?–1683) was the Puritan leader who founded Rhode Island. He was born in England.

Want to Know More?

At the Library

Avi, and James Watling (illustrator). *Finding Providence: The Story of Roger Williams.* New York: HarperCollins, 1997.

Fisher, Leonard Everett. *To Bigotry No Sanction: The Story of the Oldest Synagogue in America.* New York: Holiday House, 1998.

Hallinan, Val. *Rhode Island.* Danbury, Conn.: Children's Press, 2003.

Joseph, Paul. *Rhode Island.* Edina, Minn.: Abdo & Daughters, 1998.

Macaulay, David. *Mill.* Boston: Houghton Mifflin, 1983.

Ryan, Maria Felkins, and Linda Schmittroth (editors). *Narragansett.* San Diego, Calif.: Blackbirch, 2003.

Whitehurst, Susan. *The Colony of Rhode Island.* New York: PowerKids Press, 2000.

On the Web

Rhode Island Online
http://www.state.ri.us
To learn about Rhode Island's government and economy

Rhode Island Travel and Tourism
http://www.visitrhodeisland.com
To find out about Rhode Island's events, activities, and sights

Through the Mail

Rhode Island Tourism Division
One West Exchange Street
Providence, RI 02903
For information on travel and interesting sights in Rhode Island

Rhode Island Economic Development Corporation
One West Exchange Street
Providence, RI 02903
For information on Rhode Island's economy

Rhode Island Historical Preservation & Heritage Commission
Old State House
150 Benefit Street
Providence, RI 02903
For information on Rhode Island's historic sites

On the Road

Rhode Island State House
Smith Hill
Providence, RI 02903
401/222-2357
To visit Rhode Island's state capitol

Index

About the Author

Ann Heinrichs grew up in Fort Smith, Arkansas, and lives in Chicago. She is the author of more than one hundred books for children and young adults on Asian, African, and U.S. history and culture. Ann has also written numerous newspaper, magazine, and encyclopedia articles. She is an award-winning martial artist, specializing in t'ai chi empty-hand and sword forms.

   Ann has traveled widely throughout the United States, Africa, Asia, and the Middle East. In exploring each state for this series, she rediscovered the people, history, and resources that make this a great land, as well as the concerns we share with people around the world.